GW00792947

selecte

*Eoin Armstrong*

# repertoire
# explorer
## alto saxophone

Graded pieces for beginners

Abwechslungsreiche Spielstücke
für Anfänger

www.universaledition.com

vienna · london · new york

UE 21 486

ISMN 979-0-008-08090-6
UPC 8-03452-06448-0
ISBN 978-3-7024-6729-6

© Copyright 2009 by Universal Edition A.G., Wien

# Preface

Teachers seeking further material to enlarge their pupil's repertoire but without having to search through quantities of music that is technically too challenging for their pupil's level, need look no further.

This selection of pieces from classical to modern and studies of all kinds, is suitable for each of grades 1, 2 and 3. I have kept in mind the technical requirements for major music examinations at each level.

Whether examinations are undertaken or not, this collection presents an opportunity for any pupil in their early years of tuition to broaden their musical experiences and explore the wide variety of music that is within their grasp.

James Rae

# Vorwort

Lehrerinnen und Lehrer müssen auf der Suche nach Material, um das Repertoire ihrer Schülerinnen und Schülern zu erweitern, nun nicht mehr Unmengen von Notenheften durchstöbern, um fündig zu werden.

Diese Auswahl von klassischen bis modernen Stücken und Etüden ist geeignet für Anfänger bis leicht fortgeschrittene Spielerinnen und Spieler. Sie fand unter Berücksichtigung der Schwierigkeitsgrade des englischen Musikprüfungssystems statt.

Unabhängig davon, ob die Ausbildung nun diesem Prüfungssystem folgt oder nicht, bietet die Sammlung allen Lernenden in den ersten Jahren die Gelegenheit, den Fähigkeiten entsprechend ihre musikalischen Erfahrungen zu erweitern und eine große Vielfalt an Musikstücken zu erkunden.

James Rae

# Préface

Vous êtes enseignant et souhaitez élargir le répertoire de vos élèves sans recourir à des morceaux d'un niveau technique trop élevé ? Ne cherchez plus !

La présente sélection de pièces et études de toutes sortes, classiques et modernes, convient aux niveaux 1, 2 et 3. En faisant mon choix, j'ai aussi tenu compte des exigences techniques des examens musicaux significatifs de chaque niveau.

Que l'on choisisse ou non de gravir les échelons du système d'examens, cette sélection est pour l'élève en début d'apprentissage une occasion d'élargir le champ de son expérience musicale et d'explorer la grande variété des œuvres à sa portée.

James Rae

# Contents

# Inhalt

# Tables des matières

# Entr'acte Music from 'Rosamunde'

Franz Schubert
(1797–1828)
arr. Peter Kolman

**Grade 1**

© Copyright 1985 by Universal Edition A.G., Wien

Universal Edition  UE 21 486

# Lullaby

Johannes Brahms
(1833–1897)
arr. Peter Kolman

Grade 1

© Copyright 1985 by Universal Edition A.G., Wien

UE 21 486

**Grade 1**

# Come back, Liza

Traditional
arr. Sven Birch

© Copyright 2002 by Universal Edition A.G., Wien

UE 21 486

**Grade 1**

# Un poquito canto

Traditional
arr. Sven Birch

© Copyright 2002 by Universal Edition A.G., Wien

UE 21 486

Grade 1

play three times

# Solid Fuel

James Rae
(*1957)

Grade 1

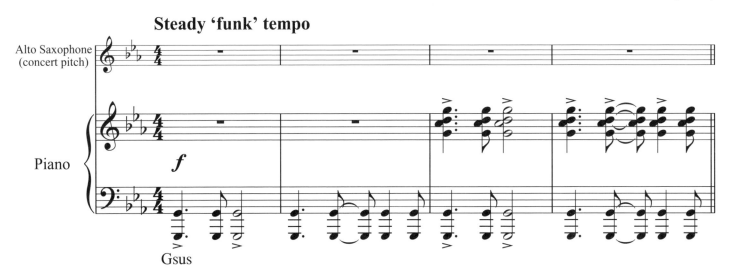

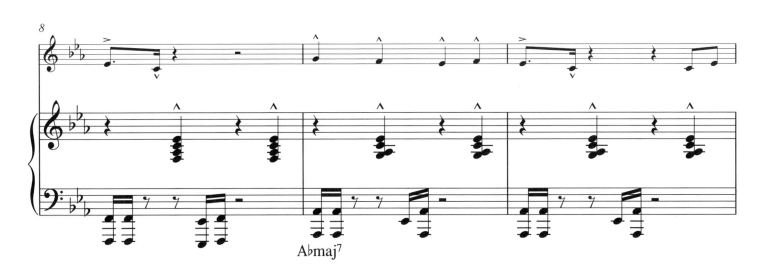

© Copyright 1997 by Universal Edition (London) Ltd., London

UE 21 486

# Rumba

James Rae
(*1957)

Grade 1

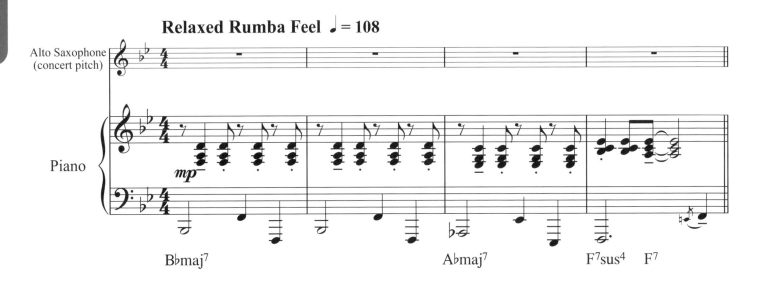

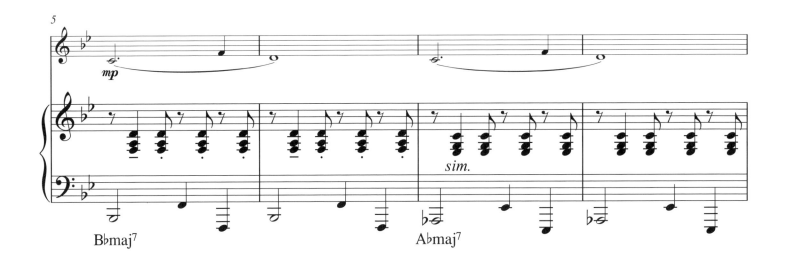

© Copyright 2002 by Universal Edition (London) Ltd., London

UE 21 486

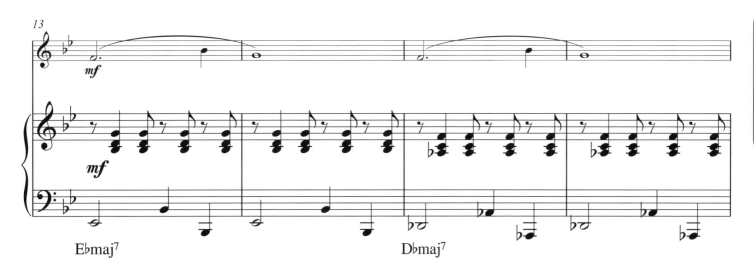

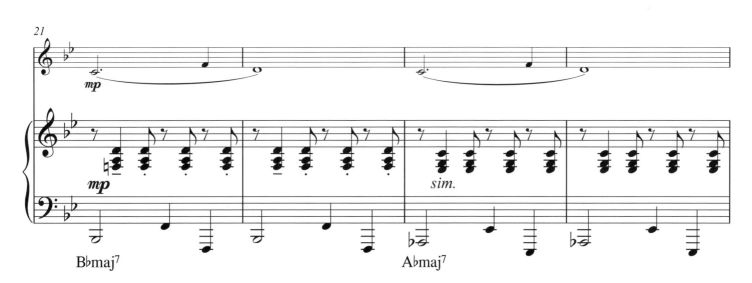

Bᵇmaj⁷    Fm⁷    Bᵇ⁷

Eᵇmaj⁷    Eᵇm⁽ᵐᵃʲ⁷⁾    Dm⁷    G⁷

Cm⁷    F⁷⁽ᵇ⁹⁾    Bmaj⁷    Bᵇmaj⁷

# Chanson triste

Pyotr Il'yich Tchaikovsky
(1840–1893)
arr. John Harle

**Grade 2**

© Copyright 1983 by Universal Edition A.G., Wien

UE 21 486

# Farewell for a Fox

Aubrey Beswick
(*1933)

**With deep feeling (♩ = ca. 104)**

© Copyright 1986 by Universal Edition (London) Ltd., London

UE 21 486

Grade 2

*to 'Mrs Sunderland' Huddersfield*

# Waltz for a Wallaby

Aubrey Beswick
(*1933)

Grade 2

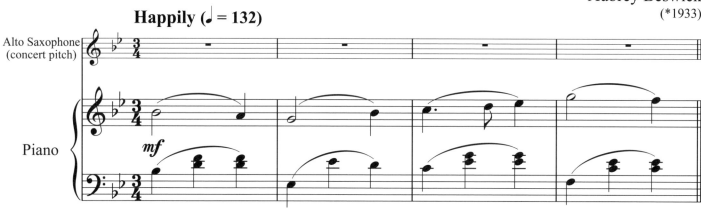

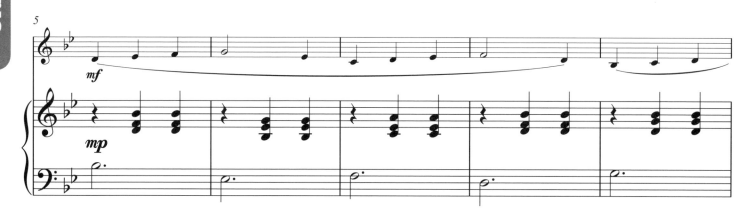

© Copyright 1986 by Universal Edition (London) Ltd., London

UE 21 486

# Rich Tune

David Bedford
(*1937)

Grade 2

© Copyright 1987 by Universal Edition (London) Ltd., London

UE 21 486

Grade 2

20

# Dorohoi Khusidl

Music: Yale Strom
(*1957)
Piano arr. Martin Reiter

**Grade 2**

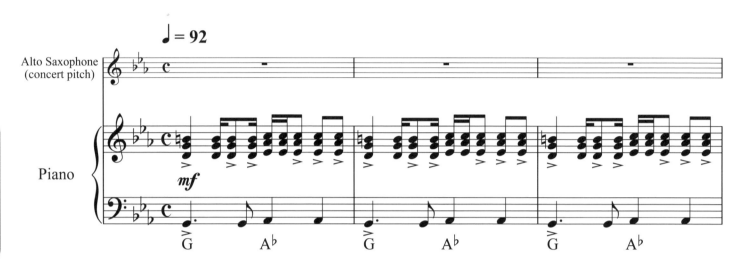

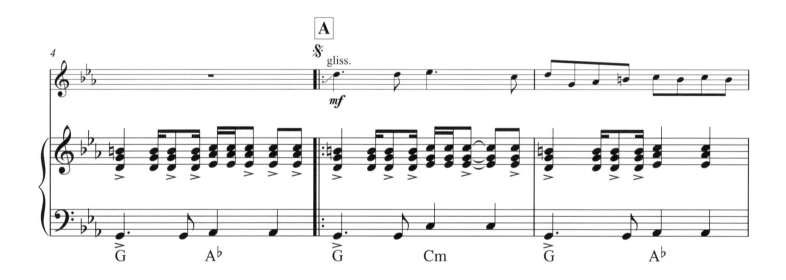

© Copyright 2004, 2008 by Universal Edition A.G., Wien

UE 21 486

# Blowin' Cool

James Rae
(*1957)

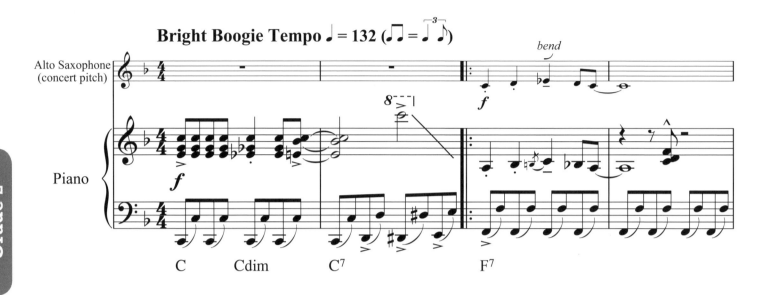

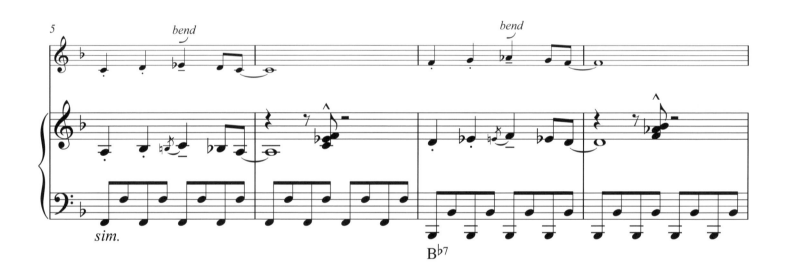

© Copyright 2002 by Universal Edition (London) Ltd., London

UE 21 486

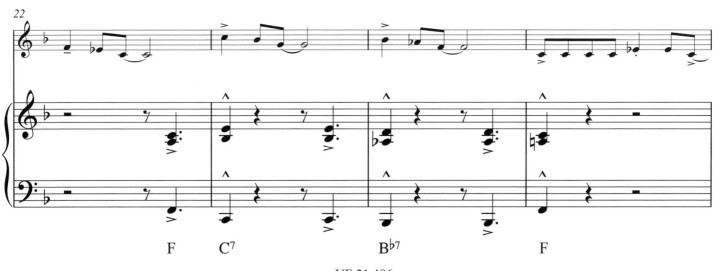

Grade 2

VACAT

Grade 2

# Minuet in G

Christian Petzold
(1677–1733)
arr. James Rae

© Copyright 1989 by Universal Edition (London) Ltd., London

UE 21 486

poco rit. (2nd time)

# Song for a Scarecrow

Aubrey Beswick
(*1933)

**Forlorn – but with a swing (♩ = ca. 108)**

© Copyright 1986 by Universal Edition (London) Ltd., London

UE 21 486

# Waltzale

David Bedford
(*1937)

**Slow waltz tempo**

© Copyright 1987 by Universal Edition (London) Ltd., London

UE 21 486

Grade 3

*) ♮ to A, 2nd time only

# Maracatu

Brazilian Traditional
arr. Jovino Santos Neto
Piano arr. Martin Reiter

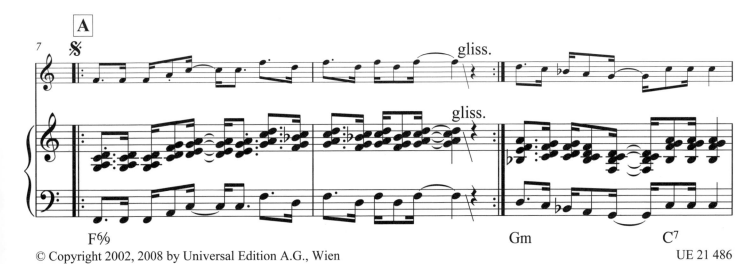

© Copyright 2002, 2008 by Universal Edition A.G., Wien

UE 21 486

34

Csus♭9 B♭6/9 A13♭9 Gm6 F6/9    Gm    C7

**B**

Csus♭9 B♭6/9 A13♭9 Gm6 F6/9  B7#11  B♭△    Am7

Fine

Gm7    Cm7 F7  B♭△    Am7 E♭△ Gm7  C7  F6/9

F6/9

UE 21 486

Grade 3

# The Silver Crown

Music: Yale Strom
(*1957)
Piano arr. Martin Reiter

© Copyright 2004, 2008 by Universal Edition A.G., Wien

UE 21 486

Grade 3

# It Don't Mean a Thing
## (if it ain't got that swing)

Duke Ellington
(1899–1974)
arr. James Rae

© 1932 (Renewed) EMI MILLS MUSIC, INC. (Publishing) and ALFRED PUBLISHING CO., INC. (Print)
This Arrangement © 2009 EMI MILLS MUSIC, INC.
All Rights Reserved including Public Performance. Used by Permission

Grade 3

Universal Edition

# A selection of saxophone titles by James Rae

## Easy

| | |
|---|---|
| Introducing the Saxophone Plus Book 1 (alto sax & pno) | UE 30 420 |
| Eyes & Ears Saxophone  Level 1 – Sight-reading (2 sax) | UE 21 144 |
| Easy Blue Saxophone (alto or tenor sax & pno) | UE 21 262 |
| Easy Jazzy Saxophone (alto or tenor sax & pno) | UE 16 578 |
| Easy Jazzy Duets  (2 sax) | UE 16 551 |
| Play it Cool – Saxophone (alto or tenor sax & pno or CD) | UE 21 100 |
| Easy Studies in Jazz and Rock (sax) | UE 19 392 |

## Easy to Intermediate

| | |
|---|---|
| Introducing the Saxophone (Engl.) (alto sax + CD) | UE 17 390 |
| James Rae's Methode für Saxophon (Dt.) (Altsax.+ CD) | UE 31 499 |
| Introducing the Saxophone Plus Book 2 (alto sax & pno) | UE 30 421 |
| Introducing Saxophone – Duets (2 sax) | UE 21 359 |
| Introducing Saxophone – Trios (3 sax) | UE 21 360 |
| Introducing Saxophone – Quartets (4 sax) | UE 21 361 |
| Eyes & Ears Saxophone  Level 2 – Sight-reading  (2 sax) | UE 21 145 |
| Style Workout – Saxophone (sax) | UE 21 232 |
| 20 Modern Studies (sax) | UE 18 820 |
| Jazz Scale Studies (sax) | UE 21 353 |
| Latin Saxophone (alto or tenor sax & pno) | UE 17 364 |
| Jazz Zone (alto or tenor sax + CD) | UE 21 030 |
| Sounds Irish (alto or tenor sax & pno) | UE 21 080 |

## Intermediate

| | |
|---|---|
| Blue Saxophone  (alto or tenor sax & pno) | UE 19 765 |
| Jazzy Saxophone 1 (alto or tenor sax & pno) | UE 18 827 |
| Jazzy Saxophone 2 (alto or tenor sax & pno) | UE 19 362 |
| Jazzy Duets (2 sax) | UE 19 395 |
| Take Ten (alto sax & pno) | UE 18 836 |
| Take Another Ten (sax & pno) | UE 21 170 |

www.universaledition.com

vienna · london · new york

654 / XII 2007